GOODBYE FLUTTERFLY

By
ANN FARNSWORTH

Jackson Trust, Publisher 2012

www.goodbyeflutterfly.com

trustee@goodbyeflutterfly.com

Early one special morning as the earth rolled deliberately through inky dark heavens, the sun crept over the horizon and steadily dispelled the night. It beamed its way over towns, across rivers and finally peeked over a window sill and into the bedroom of a little girl named Grace. As the light filtered through the window and bathed a sleepy little face, her eyes flew open; 'happy birthday to me!' Gracie whispered. She hugged the day all to herself for a minute and then hurried off to find her mother and father and sister and brothers.

A few moments later the glittering sunbeams lit up the dew in the wildness of grandmother's flower garden. The garden shimmered with light as a mother butterfly laid her cluster of precious eggs in a sanctuary underneath a broad, thick leaf. It was nearing winter and the eggs could hide safely there and wait for springs return.

Gracie paid her grandmother a birthday visit and with a pink dress and honey hair she looked just like another sweet flower to the butterflies of the garden. Grandmother and Gracie walked the garden paths and ate cake, scattering crumbs of happiness for all the wild creatures of the garden. As she was leaving Gracie waved, 'goodbye flutterflies' and it seemed all the butterflies waved right back as they floated through the air and sat prettily on their twigs and flowers.

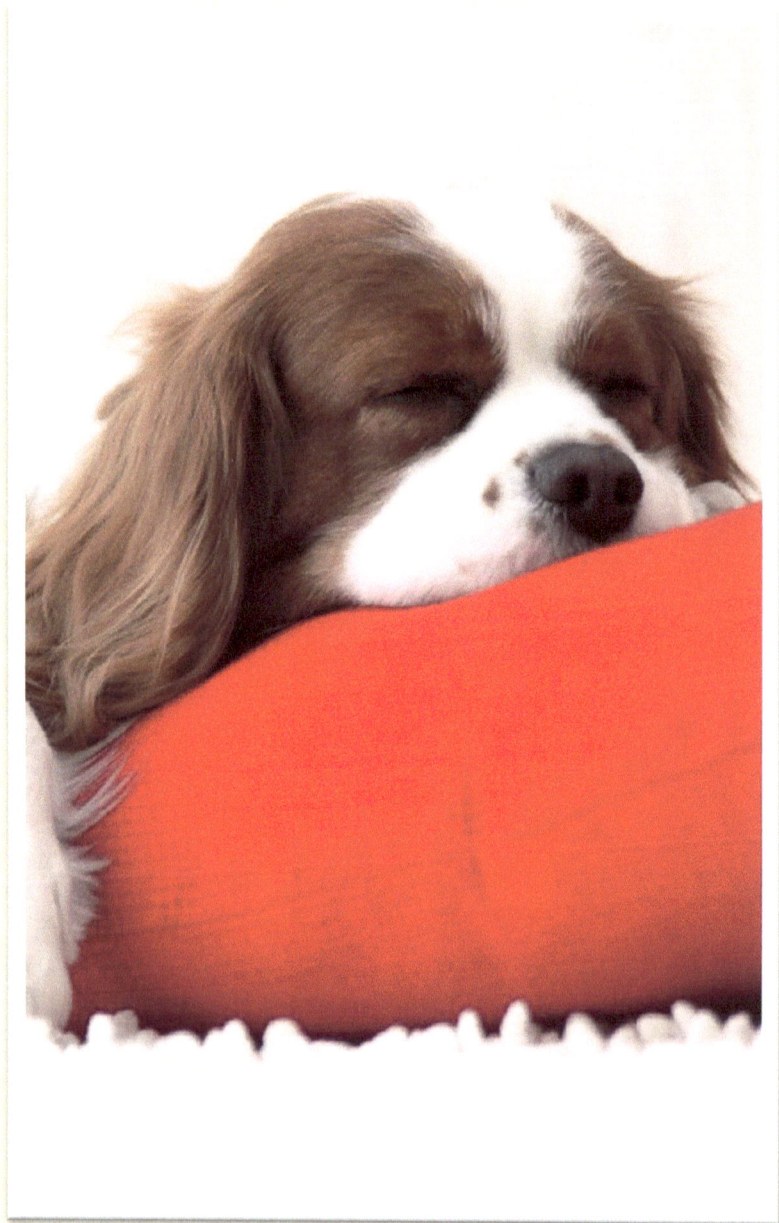

While the delicate polka dot eggs lay quietly in the garden over the winter, Gracie's family cherished every moment with their little girl. They spent afternoons at the park riding bikes and took trips to visit grandma and grandpa at their farm. They went sledding, ate snow and filled the yard with snow angels. They even bought a sleepy warm puppy.

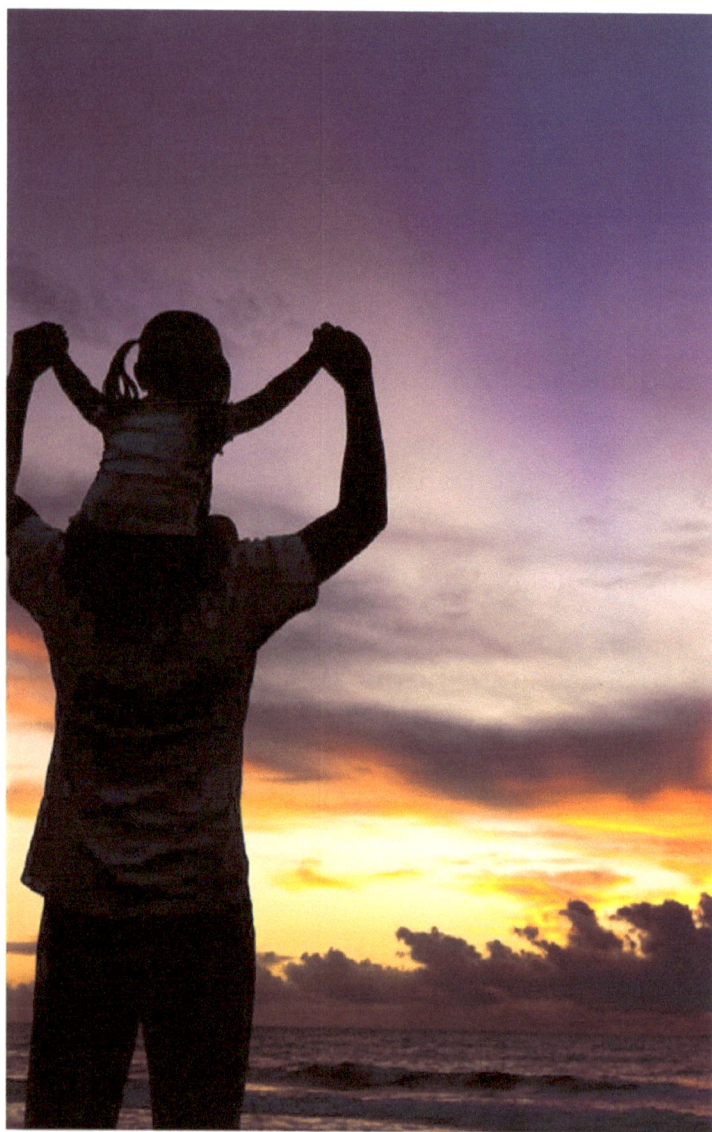

Her father held her and taught her to skate; mother made oatmeal cookies and showed her how to give butterfly kisses. Sitting on father's shoulders she was taller than her brothers and felt she could almost see forever. Gracie's family loved to make her laugh; they held her close and watched her grow.

On the day the butterfly eggs hatched, no one noticed the scrawny caterpillars crawling on the leaves in the garden. They looked too fragile to survive on their own. But even though they were small they knew what to do and they promptly began eating and growing.

While the caterpillars gained strength in the garden, mother became worried about Gracie; she seemed unsteady on her feet. It concerned her enough for a visit to the doctor and then directly to the hospital where tests showed Gracie was very ill. And though she seemed too young and so small for such a challenge, she would never be alone. She would have all the love her family could give and she would learn to be a fighter, an example to all those who encircle her with their affection.

Spring dawned early in the garden that year and the little caterpillars ate greedily, growing more and more each day. They did exactly what all caterpillars are supposed to do to grow big and strong.

racie did what children do when they face a serious illness. She trusted her parents love and put her life into the hands of trained doctors and kind nurses who worked day and night to help her in her fight.

She was patient through endless procedures. Her sister read her stories, then painted her nails and her brothers put on silliness to make her smile. Her mother and father hid their wounded and worried hope.

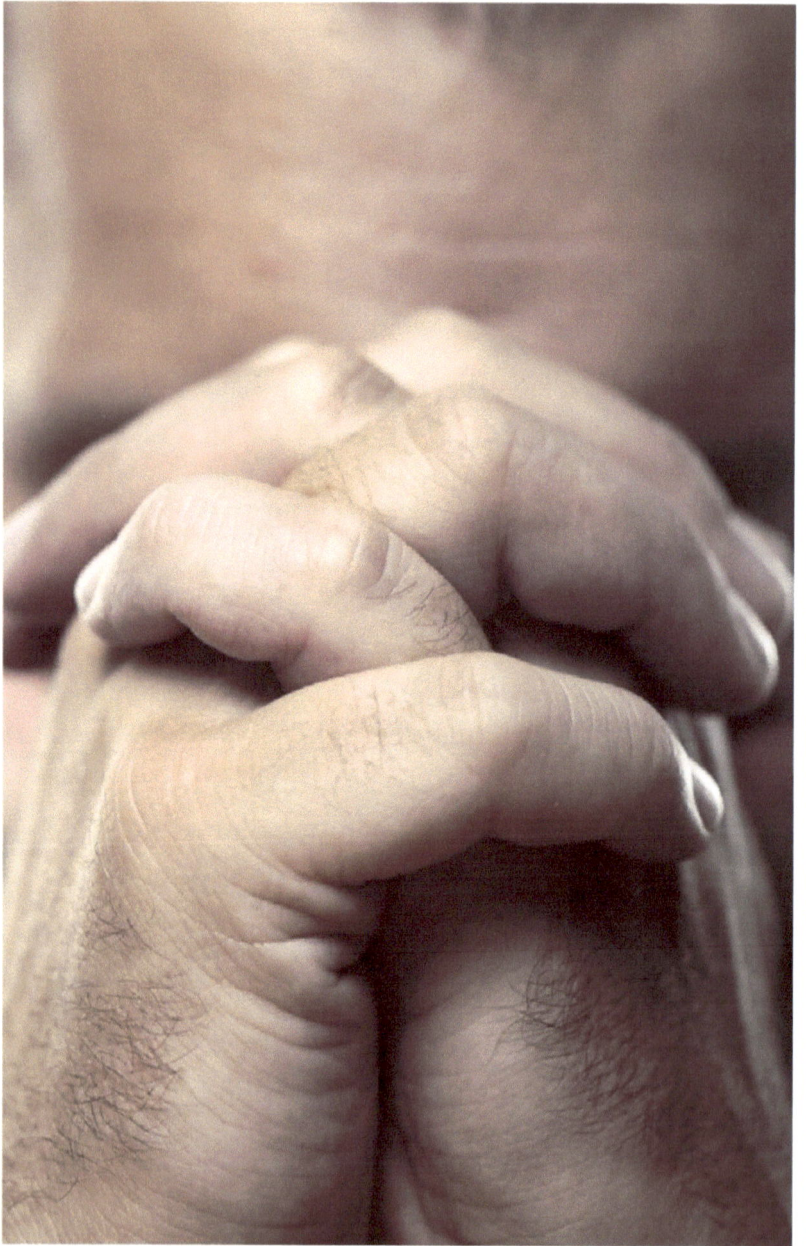

They all prayed to that One who hears our prayers and He kept them constantly in His tender care.

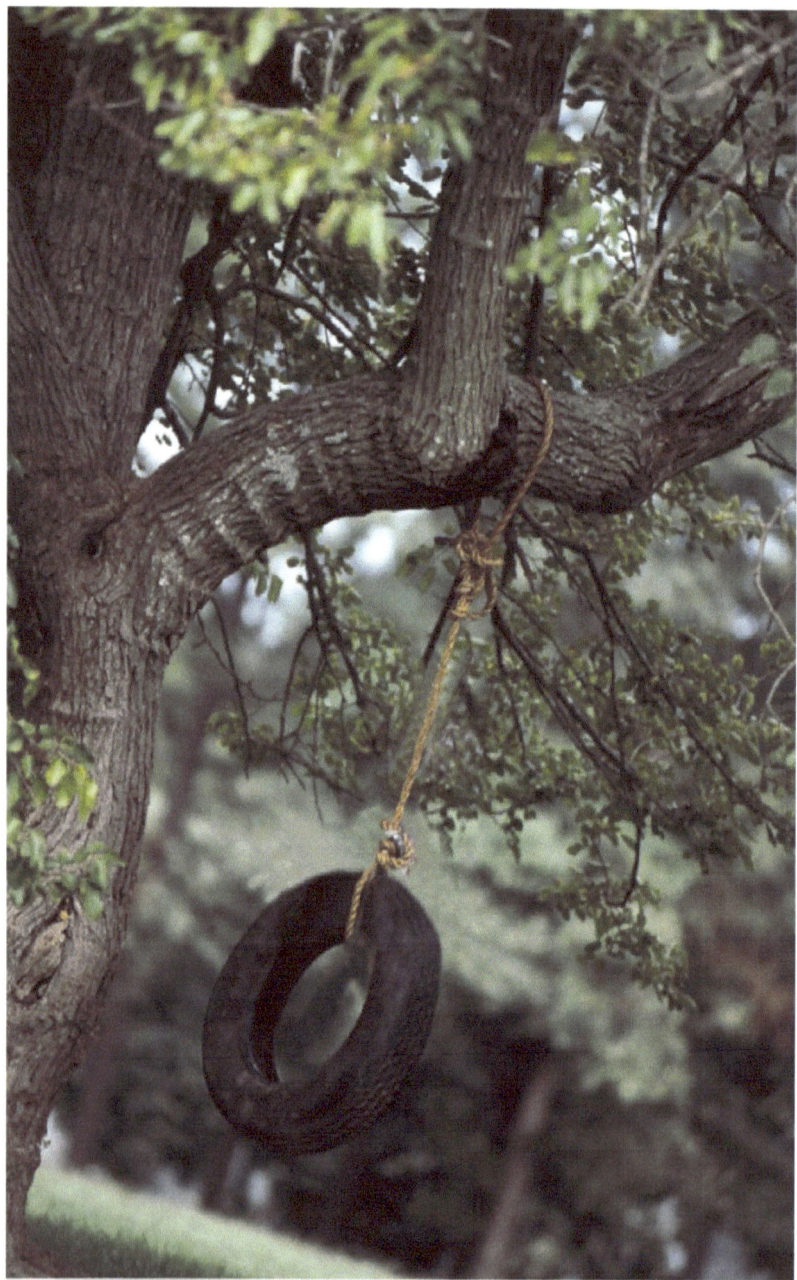

When the caterpillar had eaten its way through the garden, it found a branch high in a tree the children loved to climb, a sheltered spot where it began spinning a cocoon. It first attached itself fast to the tree and then spun its silken thread around and around until it was wrapped in a puffy tangle, sure and safe. There the hungry caterpillar began a marvelous journey. It would ultimately emerge as a heavenly destined butterfly. This was the intention from the very beginning; the caterpillar wasn't created to remain earth bound. It was carefully placed on a path to become a heavenly creature.

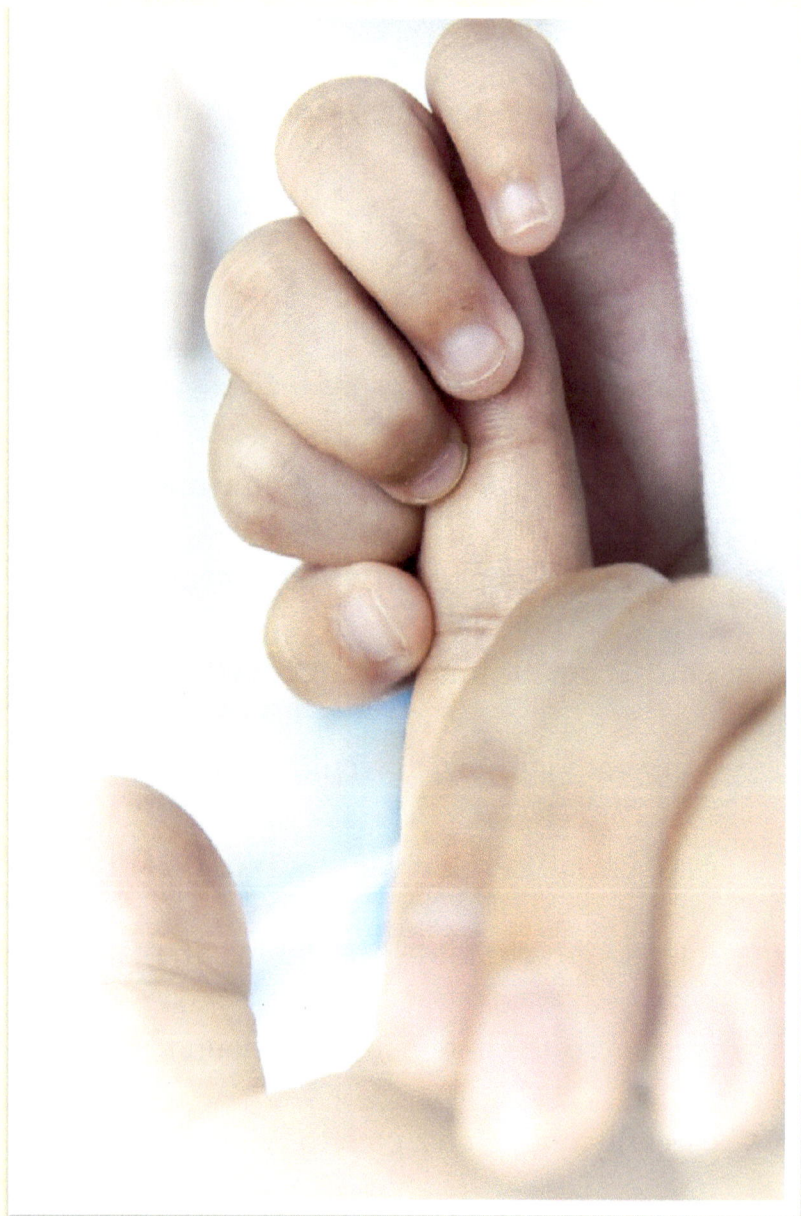

Gracie, wrapped securely in her family's love, now rested. She had been helped in every way and now they waited to see how their treasured child would emerge from this great ordeal. Gracie was a valiant fighter, she rested and ate, but her small body grew weaker and more frail. One night while lying in her mother's arms she whispered, "Mother, I just want to go and play." Her parents felt the coming change, and with broken hearts they let her go.

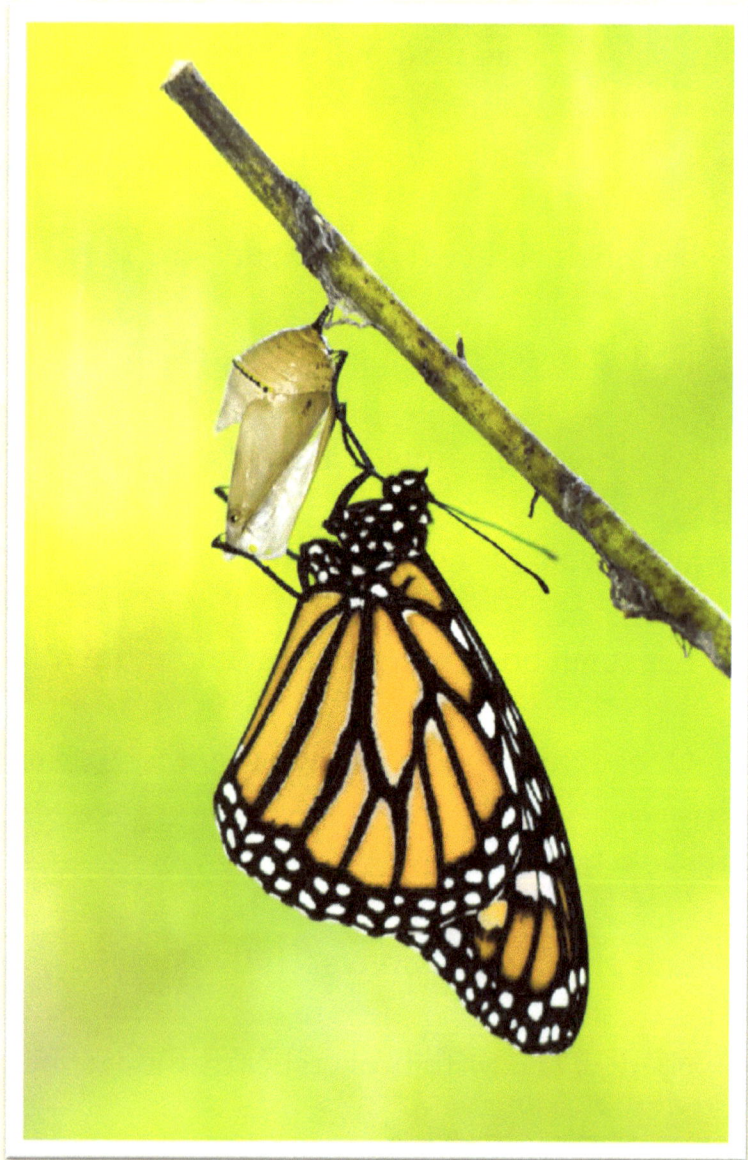

Early that morning a new butterfly pushed and struggled free from the protective cocoon that had been warmed by the rays of a golden sun. Strength pumped into its brilliantly colored wings and unfurling, the butterfly prepared for first flight. The sun's light caught the jeweled facets of translucent wings, a snapshot of a glorious creation. In just a breath the butterfly, spreading wings wide to catch the wind, took off and flew high in the garden sky. It fluttered and hovered and floated, discovering sights and wonders unseen while tethered to an earthly form.

Leaving her body behind, Gracie's spirit took flight, watching over her family with a complete and abiding love, soaring to greater lights, happy reunions and new adventures. Gracie didn't need to say goodbye, her world now includes the upper reaches of the garden. Traveling ahead of those she loves, she watches over them with greater understanding. Like the butterfly she is now in a bright and vivid world and with this new vision she says to them "Look up, little caterpillar, and look forward to the richness of this world above the garden."

Many hearts ache while missing Gracie. But there are occasions when the world is perfectly quiet and still, that they feel her close. They sense her near and feel the love of a sweet butterfly kiss whispering softly on their cheek.

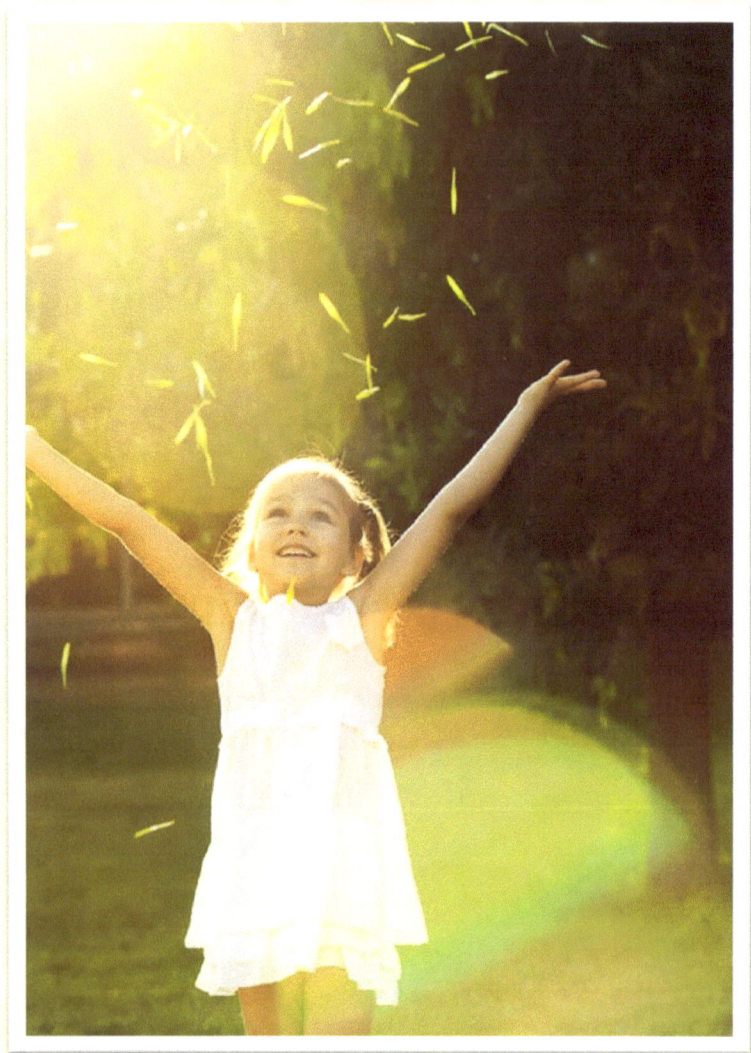

They will not have to miss her long.

Are we not all traveling the same course as the diligent caterpillar, feasting in God's earthly garden and looking forward to the day we emerge from this mortal journey transformed into His finished creation? We can be sure as we grow and mature in this part of the garden that we are becoming what we were intended to be. Certain that there will be someone waiting to welcome us even as Gracie will be anxiously waiting, happy to be forever with loved ones in their new and joyous home.

www.ingramcontent.com/pod-product-compliance
Lightning Source LLC
LaVergne TN
LVHW010036070426
835513LV00005B/124